Dogs

Bloodhounds

by Connie Colwell Miller

Consulting Editor: Gail Saunders-Smith, PhD

Consultant: Jennifer Zablotny, DVM
Member, American Veterinary Medical Association

Capstone *press*

Mankato, Minnesota

12/11

Pebble Books are published by Capstone Press,
151 Good Counsel Drive, P.O. Box 669, Mankato, Minnesota 56002.
www.capstonepress.com

1 2 3 4 5 6 12 11 10 09 08 07

Library of Congress Cataloging-in-Publication Data
Miller, Connie Colwell, 1976–
   Bloodhounds / by Connie Colwell Miller.
   p. cm.—(Pebble Books. Dogs)
   Summary: "Simple text and photographs present the bloodhound breed and
how to care for them"—Provided by publisher.
   Includes bibliographical references and index.
   ISBN-13: 978-0-7368-6698-9 (hardcover)
   ISBN-10: 0-7368-6698-1 (hardcover)
   1. Bloodhound—Juvenile literature. I. Title. II. Series.
SF429.B6M55 2007
636.753'6—dc22   2006020382

Note to Parents and Teachers

The Dogs set supports national science standards related to life science. This book describes and illustrates bloodhounds. The images support early readers in understanding the text. The repetition of words and phrases helps early readers learn new words. This book also introduces early readers to subject-specific vocabulary words, which are defined in the Glossary section. Early readers may need assistance to read some words and to use the Table of Contents, Glossary, Read More, Internet Sites, and Index sections of the book.

Table of Contents

Nosy Dogs

Bloodhounds have powerful noses. Bloodhounds sometimes focus on a smell and forget everything else.

Bloodhounds help police.
They follow scent trails.
They help find
missing people.

Bloodhounds are
gentle dogs.
They do not bite the
people they sniff out.
They bark to show
what they found.

From Puppy to Adult

Bloodhound puppies like to sniff out smelly things. Owners should watch these busy puppies carefully.

Young bloodhounds
are clumsy and messy.
They grow quickly
from small puppies
to large dogs.

Adult bloodhounds
are big and tall.
Their loose skin looks
too large for their strong
bodies. Drool drips
from their big lips.

Bloodhound Care

Bloodhounds need
a lot of exercise.
They enjoy walking
through woods full
of interesting smells.

Bloodhounds can have stomach problems. They should rest after eating. Owners should feed them a few small meals each day.

Bloodhounds need
patient owners with lots
of time to care for them.
Bloodhounds are
loyal pets.

Glossary

clumsy—careless and awkward in movements

drool—spit that drips from the mouth

focus—to keep all your attention on one thing

patient—calm during frustrating or difficult times

scent—the smell of something

Read More

Murray, Julie. *Bloodhounds.* Dogs. Edina, Minn.: Abdo, 2003.

Wilcox, Charlotte. *The Bloodhound.* Learning about Dogs. Mankato, Minn.: Capstone Press, 2001.

Internet Sites

FactHound offers a safe, fun way to find Internet sites related to this book. All of the sites on FactHound have been researched by our staff.

Here's how:

1. Visit *www.facthound.com*
2. Choose your grade level.
3. Type in this book ID **0736866981** for age-appropriate sites. You may also browse subjects by clicking on letters, or by clicking on pictures and words.
4. Click on the **Fetch It** button.

FactHound will fetch the best sites for you!

Index

Word Count: 147
Grade: 1
Early-Intervention Level: 17

Editorial Credits
Martha E. H. Rustad, editor; Juliette Peters, set designer; Kyle Grenz, book designer;
Kara Birr, photo researcher; Scott Thoms, photo editor

Photo Credits
Capstone Press/Karon Dubke, 12, 18; Cheryl A. Ertelt, 10; Kent Dannen, cover, 8;
Mark Raycroft, 1; Photo by Fiona Green, 14; Ron Kimball Stock/Ron Kimball, 4, 16;
Shutterstock/Laurie Lindstrom, 20; www.jeanmfogle.com, 6